LOVE
BEYOND ALL TELLING

An Introduction to the Mystery of God

by
Sr Una O'Connor, IBVM
&
Fr Brian Grogan, SJ

IRISH MESSENGER PUBLICATIONS
37 Lower Leeson Street,
Dublin 2.

Waiting

Why is there a space?
Is there going to be another guest?
Is your happiness complete as long as this place remains empty?
It has always been waiting there and
They have always been waiting.
They are waiting for you
As if there were only you in the world.
You are precious in Their eyes.
Yes? You live in the Trinity who lives in you:
You are Their guest and They are your Guests.
Let your Three Guests love each other within you,
Praise each other in you and
Sing of each other.
Let Them dance for joy in your tent.
Our secret is that They are in us:
Let us become aware of this
In the land of silence.

INTRODUCING GOD

Students of Mystery

A nine-year-old was being cajoled by his mother into finishing his dinner. "There are hundreds of children who would love to have that food!", she argued. The boy looked with distaste at his plate, then glared at his mother and said: "Name three of them!"

Such a child might on another occasion embarrass his mother again by asking her, in the company of other adults, "Tell me all about God!" It can be hard to talk about God, despite the fact that we think about Him and use the name 'God' frequently. This booklet is written to help us find words to use about God, to help us to be able to hold a mature conversation about Him. Taking up the boy's demand to 'name three of them', we will be exploring the mystery of the Three Persons in God, because to reach into the world of God is to touch on mystery immediately.

This is a booklet to be read slowly. Once you find a passage that makes sense to you and satisfies you, please stay with it and relish that part. You might find it helpful to mark the bits that mean something special to you. Make them your own; use them in prayer, when you speak directly to God and listen to Him. If you have a group or a friend with whom you can share about God, try chatting out the parts that make sense to you and puzzle together over the more obscure parts.

Mystery can have various effects on us. The mystery of evil frightens us. Mathematical mysteries can frustrate us and make us feel small and inadequate and perhaps stupid, but then there are many mysteries which are puzzling yet attractive. The mysteries of nature, of the stars and the universe these we do not fully understand yet we are drawn to them. They are bigger than ourselves, yet they give us a sense of wonder and delight. For a child everything in the world around it is a source of wonder and fascination. This sense of wonder, curiosity and desire to understand is a divine gift to the child otherwise it would never learn and grow. A growing child wants to get to the bottom of everything. This desire will run from exploring the mystery of its own toes to dismantling a T.V. set. Sadly, the sense of wonder, and of desire to explore everything gets lost in much of to-day's education: knowledge is pushed in, rather than curiosity and wonder being drawn out. Yet the hunger remains and can be brought to life.

The Attraction of Mystery

See what effect this story has on you! A woman went to work in a remote village on the Chile/Peru border. While there, the villagers often talked in muted voices about the "cave of mysteries". At the end of her stay, they invited her to travel to it: this was their parting gift to her. A party of seven left the village long before dawn one morning and travelled into the hills for two hours, arriving finally at a quiet lake. They boarded a boat which was moored at the edge of the water. The leader took his place at the prow and began to pull at a rope which stretched across the lake. All this was done in total silence. The boat glided across the water noiselessly towards rocks on the far side. As they neared their destination, a narrow opening appeared and the boat moved into a dark cave and slowly stopped. In the eerie darkness, lights began to appear, first here and there, then all over the roof of the cave. In the light could be seen the colours of the rocks. Stalactites and stalagmites glowed with luminous splendour. Then one of the group coughed. Immediately the lights went out and they were plunged into total darkness. The boat began to move and they found themselves emerging on to the lake again. They moored in silence and walked back in Indian file to the village without saying a word. The woman, unable to restrain her curiosity any longer, went to the leader and asked what it all meant. "The cave is inhabited by an unusual species of glow-worm", she was told. "In total silence they light up but if there is any noise, they hide themselves by ceasing to glow". This story illustrates the fact that mystery can be attractive, that it can draw us out of ourselves and give us a sense of delight.

We seem to be made for mystery — why else did Agatha Christie become so popular? Our focus in the first part of this booklet will be on some aspects of the mystery we find in persons, the mystery in you and in those around you. For behind every mystery, and especially the mystery of persons, stands God. As children grow to adulthood, their primary interest shifts from the mystery of things to the mystery of persons. They become fascinated by themselves and want to know more about themselves and about others. The natural world retains its capacity to enchant them but the human world, with all its interplay of persons, begins to become endlessly fascinating. Why is this? Isn't it because persons are unpredictable, full of mystery?

"Will You Marry Us?"

Falling in love is a delightful and inexhaustible experience of mystery. Who could have predicted the outcome of the following encounter between a priest, working in Somalia with refugees, and three Somali young ladies? He watched them as they tried out a Polaroid camera they had just acquired. They were delighted with themselves. Then one of them came over to him, showed him one of the snaps and asked in all simplicity, "Am I not very beautiful?" He nodded affirmatively. She showed other snaps with the same approval. Then she asked about his wife and, under her steady questioning, he admitted he had none. She paused, then said, "We three will be your wives. You will marry us and take us from here to your own country. You will care for us and we three will look after you always!" His head swimming, the priest could only manage to say: "In my country it is not allowed to have three wives; only one. What if I wished to marry just you alone?" The maiden looked at her companions, then at the ground and finally replied, "No, it cannot be. We three are friends and we have made an agreement". "What agreement?", he asked weakly. "We promised that we would always stay together and that all three of us would marry the one man, or else that we would never marry!" And beckoning to her companions they walked away and he never saw them again.

There is mystery here: the mystery of what goes on in the human heart in relation to other persons. Our point in touching on the mystery of human persons is to open up the guidelines that lead to appreciation of the Divine Persons. God is Mystery but so are we. If we follow through on the mysterious aspects of ourselves, we come to appreciate the mystery of the Divine Persons. What the Somali maiden said of her companions turns out to be even more wonderfully true of God: each of the Three Divine Persons says to us: "We three are friends and we can never be separated. When one of us comes to you in love, we all come to you and we look after you always".

The Words we Use

Over the last number of years, you have probably become aware of the sexist language that is used generally, and also in our speaking of God. There is a growing openness among people and especially among women, to the fact that God encompasses the best of masculine and feminine gifts. Jesus, as a human person, is seen by many as the complete person embodying the ideal set of male and female qualities.

When we think of femininity, we think of qualities like life-giving intimacy, nurturing, empathy, sensitivity to the needs of others, thoughtfulness, community bonding, compassion. God relates to us with all these qualities and so our appreciation of God grows from our human experience of these qualities in ourselves and in those around us. Perhaps the Holy Spirit can be said to be the Person of the Trinity who reveals the feminine in God. It is He (or She!) who works in our hearts to develop all the qualities mentioned above and to develop them to the fullest.

Having briefly addressed ourselves to this issue, we have chosen to stay with the traditional 'He' in referring to all the Persons of the Trinity.

Introducing Friends

The sub-title of this work is 'An Introduction to the Mystery of God'. Think of yourself as wanting to introduce your best friend to someone else. Let's say you have fallen in love and that you decide to bring your beloved home to your family. Let's imagine too that you have happy, family relationships and that perhaps your parents have been urging you to bring your beloved home. You'll be hoping that the event will go well and that the family will receive your friend and appreciate him or her. At the very least, you hope that there won't be rejection on either side. Beyond that, you'll be hoping that something of the worth and value of your friend may come across, that something of what you have seen in your friend and which has made you happy and has brightened your life, may come across to the family.

And yet, all you can do is make the introductions and then hope for the best. The process is largely outside your control. You try to set up the situation as best you can but then the relationship either takes off, or fails to do so. If the overtures go well, you will later set up other situations to foster the relationship. Your parents come to a level of appreciation of your friend that is independent of you and are glad to have that friend around even if you're not there. If you marry the friend, it may be that in twenty or thirty years' time you'll be building on a little flat because you and your partner have agreed to care for your mother and father in their declining years.

This is perhaps a somewhat idealised picture of the transition over long years from tentative introduction to the full flowering of friendship. Nevertheless, it serves our purpose. It gives an image of how our relationship with God can develop. What Jesus was intent on throughout his public life was on introducing people to His Father. All he wanted to do was to make him known. "No one has ever seen God; it is the only Son, who is nearest to the Father's heart, who has made Him known" (John 1:18). This Gospel is essentially an introduction of the Three Divine Persons in relationship with One Another and with the world.

The Father

The desire of Jesus' heart was that we would comprehend the sort of person the Father is. His greatest fear and sorrow was that the One he loved, valued and appreciated most would be rejected. He was always puzzling out ways to make the introductions better. All the parables were efforts to show what a wonderful and surprising and loving person the Father is. His teachings, such as the Sermon on the Mount, were efforts to reveal His Father's heart, His values and attitudes. Likewise, His miracles were efforts to reveal the lavish goodness of the Father. His concern for our well-being, his power to help us. For most people, the Passion and Resurrection proved to be the best of all introductions to the Father by Jesus. In accepting His Passion, Jesus showed how important He considered His Father's wishes to be: He wanted the Father to be free to show in Himself how much He loved our world, and so He was open to whatever the Father asked of Him. "I have finished the work that you gave me to do . . . I have made your name known" (John 17:4-5).

The Son

But, in fact, the interplay between Father and Son was such that not only did Jesus reveal the Father and the Father's heart to the world, but the Father introduced the Son throughout His public life to us. He introduced Him at the Baptism and told us who He was. "This is My Son, the Beloved; My favour rests on Him" (Matthew 3:17) and repeated the introduction at the Transfiguration (Matthew 17:5).

In a sense, in all the miracles, the Father was trying to tell us about the Son. The miracles were worked through the Father's power; they were approbation of Jesus by the Father, inviting us to focus on Jesus and know Him better. Finally, the Resurrection was the most complete introduction by the Father, as if the Father were saying: "Now you know My Son properly. By My raising this Man

8

from the dead I am telling you who He truly is, My Beloved Son, equal to Myself: everything He has said about Me and about His own relationship to Me is true!"

The Spirit

When we read in St John's Gospel about Jesus introducing the Holy Spirit, it helps to be aware that the Spirit was listening to what Jesus was saying about Him. He knew the role He had to play and was totally committed to it. In pointing out the importance of Jesus for the world, He also pointed out the glory of the Father. The Son revealed the Father, the Spirit revealed the Son, and the Son revealed the Spirit. Thus, there was one complex revelation by which the truth of God as Three Persons became known. Father sent Son, Father and Son together sent the Spirit and, since no one sends oneself on a mission, the Three must be distinct Persons.

Jesus gave His first hint about the Spirit by speaking of Him as a fountain of living water. This would have intrigued the Jews who were praying for rain at the time (John 7:38). At the Last Supper, He named Him as the Spirit of Truth who would make known the hidden depths of the mystery of Jesus and the meaning of all He did. He will be on your side; He will intercede for you and defend you! So closely were Son and Spirit united that both Jesus' last breath and the water from His side were tokens of the outpouring of the Spirit. In His Resurrection, Jesus completed the introductions. He breathed on the disciples — another symbol of the giving of the Spirit — and then presented Him, saying: "Receive the Holy Spirit" (John 20:22). Note Jesus' confidence throughout. He did not say that he *hoped* that the Spirit would undo sin, make all things new and so complete the work His Father and He had done. No, there was a certainty of success here, as if Father and Son had said: "We are sending our best person; He will get the job done. Trust Him!"

Three Persons

At the Resurrection, of course, it was as if the Three Divine Persons had come crowding in together, for it was then the Spirit came openly into our world, to join the Father and Son in Their abiding presence with us till the close of human history and beyond.

The great revelation of the New Testament is that God is not one Person but Three, and that the Three are totally in love with us and want to share their family life with us. They are determined to spare no effort to reveal Their love and to invite us in.

"Over to You!"

Jesus chose to enlist His followers to continue the introductions after His lifetime. You have probably been introduced to God in many ways but the introductions may not have been followed up and so the relationship languished and failed to advance from light acquaintance to a firm and lasting friendship that would have become central to your life and have given meaning and purpose to it all. Or perhaps, the introductions went well and a good level of friendship developed. But some misunderstanding may have arisen and the growth in the relationship was stultified. What most often occurs is that the cold wind of evil blows across our warm and easy friendship and we begin to doubt that God is really good. We attribute evil to Him: "Why did God do that to me? If He really cared, why did He allow that tragedy?"

If this little booklet can help even a small number of people renew their relationship with God, or develop it more fully, then it will have been worthwhile.

"How can I?"

You can enhance your relationship with God by talking it over with Him in personal prayer; by reading the New Testament for yourself, since it is the primary source for our knowing God; and by pondering reflectively over your own life and its details, and coming to recognise the presence of God in it. Then, of course, there are the Sacraments, in which we meet God directly under many different symbols.

According as you come to know God more, you can experience the joy of sharing Him with others. There is a special joy in speaking about God; try it and you will notice it. It is a glimmer in us of what the Three Divine Persons experience in revealing One another to us. Jesus had this joy and He wants it for us too.

Perhaps you need to be convinced that you have a role to play in introducing God to others. Many lay people feel that they know so little *about* God that they should leave it to the experts to speak of Him. And, indeed, the official Church often thwarts the diligent efforts of some of the laity to take a greater part in evangelisation. Yet God seems to have fewer problems about this than the 'official' Church and He entrusts parents with the task and joy of introducing Him to their children.

Get to know the Person!

The central thing is not knowledge *about* because when introducing another person it is not knowing *about* the person that matters so much as knowing the person directly. A story goes of the famous singer who came to a small town and gave a recital. After singing *The Lord is My Shepherd* there was quiet applause. It was indeed well sung. Then someone told the singer that one of the village men in the audience often sang that hymn. The singer graciously invited the local to perform. At the end there was rapturous applause. The travelling performer was puzzled. He realized that although the local's technique was deficient, he had put a quality into the song that he himself lacked. The local man said gently to him: "You know the song, but I know the Shepherd!"

10

Why Bother?

We hope what is written in this booklet may help you, both to know more about God and to know Him directly through love, for love is *the* form of knowledge. We only know people truly when we love them. Knowledge of persons is born of love. We try to show the loveableness of God here, not because it is totally unknown to you, but because you can grow endlessly in appreciation of its length and depth; for it is infinite and always new and surprising and attractive. But someone might say: "Why bother? All this labour to know God more . . . is it worth it? Let's watch television or play golf". In reply, first let it be said that there is much religious indifference abroad these days. In times past, people killed one another over issues of faith. Now there is a sense of apathy: "God is not worth making a fuss over". There is a form of practical atheism around too, born perhaps out of a dissatisfaction with the ways in which religion is presented through the Churches. God has become irrelevant; sincere and dedicated people shelve Him and turn their attention and energies to the more practical issues of justice.

Then the cult of affluence, materialism, consumerism, plays its part. Practical comforts are more tangible than divine concerns and the focus of concern becomes shorter.

Why bother? The question touches the deepest issues of human existence. What does it mean to be human? Why are we here? What is life all about? St Augustine, having tried many alternatives, came up with the conviction that God has made us for Himself and that our hearts are restless until they rest in Him. St Thomas Aquinas, eight centuries later, asked where human happiness is to be found? Not in wealth or power or . . .

In Search of Happiness   *In search of meaning*

You can verify in your own experience the claim of psychologists today: when interpersonal relationships are good, people can be truly happy even if they are poor or ill or whatever. Happiness lies in good relationships with other persons. The most significant persons, the best of persons are those who truly understand us and who love us limitlessly, who see the best in us when we do not see it. They are persons who forgive us and encourage and inspire us, who make us feel at home, who share with us the best they have. We may meet such persons and we are blessed if we do. At our best, we may be trying to be like this to others.

Behind the goodness in others and in ourselves stand the silent Three who are the authors of all human goodness. We are to share Their joy, Their happiness. Better still, we are made to *become* that joy and happiness in some way: we and all our fellow-humans. We are made to know God in this sense; not simply to have lots of 'head' knowledge of God but to have knowledge that is born of love. We have, collectively, a desire for the infinite. We have an ultimate concern that stretches beyond all our finite concerns. This ultimate concern turns out to be personal, a community of Persons. Slowly we must learn to focus on Them; otherwise life remains empty and unfulfilled no matter what we pile into it.

Why bother? Ask first, why bother to enter into a relationship with any other person? Pondering this will reveal that we have a need for others. We cannot exist or be happy alone. Our need for others to love and be loved by them is but a faint echo of our need for a similar relationship of mutual love for The Others.

"Tell Them Who I Am!"

In a mysterious way, God waits for us to introduce Him to one another. Why He should do this is a mystery, since we may so easily fail in our task, either by ignoring it or doing it badly. Why did God delay so long before beginning to reveal Himself to the human race in Judaism? Why wait so long before sending the Son and the Spirit to complete the revelation of God as Trinity, the revelation of Three Divine Persons totally in love with us in all our misery and evil? We do not know. What does matter is that we, here and now, respond to Their endless invitation to come to know Them better. Why would we not wish to know better someone who seems to love us through and through, whose dreams and intentions for us are the best, whose only desire is for our happiness? Such are They, who lavish infinite attention on us, who invite us endlessly yet gently, who labour for us in all events, turning them at whatever cost, to our good.

What about the World?

We are writing for people who are concerned about the world. Such people often legitimately ask: "Will all the reflections in this booklet change the situation of the poor or the oppressed? And if they don't, why not wait until the next life to find out all about God? Let's devote our time and energy in this life to direct service of those who need our help". This point of view is to be taken seriously. Many Christians cultivate a relationship with God and seem to ignore the plight of the needy. Their spirituality seems privatised, self-satisfying. What about the world, indeed?

Our position is as follows: the spirituality or way of proceeding proposed and lived out by Jesus, is one of radical concern for others, even unto death. Gospel spirituality is totally incarnational: it accepts the world situation as it is and refuses to flinch from its evil aspects; it involves itself fully in the human condition through vulnerable love and humble service; foot-washing is the Gospel image for that service (John 13:4-11).

Such service does not exhaust Jesus' gift to the world. He is the one who best knows His Father, so He knows the Father's dream for us; He knows what we are to become. We are not simply to be creatures of this world, needing help to make our brief history on this little planet a less painful one. The Father's dream stretches to infinite horizons. He wants to have us as His eternal companions. God became human so that human beings could become God — so said the early Church. Grasp rightly what the human race is to be and then there is hope that you will serve it rightly out of a faith-vision which is really an acceptance of God's own vision of humanity. From this will emerge an active love which will express itself in work for justice that is both passionate and wise at once.

Getting Involved

When you come to know God as He truly is, you will be fired by His vision for the world. You will find in yourself an energy to play your part in the growth of the world towards God. The vision and love that inspired the Son will inspire you. You will take your cue from Him; you will keep your eye firmly fixed on Him; your standards for involvement in our sordid, pathetic yet marvellous world will be His standards rather than those which others find acceptable. All of this is radically transforming.

Growing to know God involves an altering of vision: a shift of values from the merely human to the infinitely rich values of God. From that shift, there emerges a new set of attitudes: a mind-set that often runs counter to the thinking of people around you and a responsiveness to the calls and demands of the Gospel that knows no limits. Faith shifts from being a well-defined set of holy facts, for you could on one level believe the Creed and yet be an enemy of humanity. Religion shifts from being a well-ordered set of gestures: "I never miss Mass", "I fast", "I pay my dues . . ." etc. towards a relationship of love, vibrant and full of surprises. This new relationship also makes demands. It is not static but dynamic. Self-displacement and self-transcendence occur. You are drawn out of yourself, you find yourself being drawn beyond any boundaries you had decided on; you lose yourself and yet, strangely, you find a new and better self. Falling in love is like that. Falling in love with God involves falling in love with humanity.

The Risk of Loving

After being introduced to God, you will, if all goes well, find yourself swept off your feet and hear yourself saying 'Yes' to all sorts of divine invitations which bring you closer both to the Three Divine Persons and to all other persons as well. By being with Them you are with all Their friends as well. You are 'with' everyone, and anyone may become your neighbour at any moment with a legitimate claim to your help and your love. It is in this way that God continually enlists us to take on our share of His task of bringing the world to Himself. We are to embody God in our place and time, for the saving of the world. God works along by establishing relationships. One by one we are introduced to Him; a relationship is initiated and nurtured, and is open to endless growth. It then becomes our role to establish good relationships with others.

It will be a joy and a blessing if we can introduce people to God in some way. If that is not directly possible, we can bring God into their lives by loving them rightly, for God is love. The task of forging loving relationships across space and time become a cooperative venture between the Three Divine Persons and ourselves. We become co-responsible with Them for the well-being of the world and its evolution to its destined glory.

Mystery and Growth

In continuing your exploration into this mystery, remember that it will be a personal journey for you because it is all about personal relationships. Let the mystery carry you along. It is not so much a matter of understanding but of being attracted. Let it appeal to your heart rather than to your head. Allow the mystery of it all evoke attitudes of reverence and awe in you, as though you were looking at a beautiful sunset. There is nothing to be done about a sunset. It is there to be accepted gratefully and pondered. We can carry a mystery around with us and gradually it unfolds more and more.

There can be mystery without growth as is seen in the story of a boy being examined by a bishop during a Confirmation ceremony. The bishop asked, "How many Persons in God?" The boy replied, "Three Persons in one God". The bishop chose to look bewildered and said, "But I don't understand how there can be three Persons in one God". The boy looked him in the eye and replied, "My Lord, you are not meant to understand!" Again, in a practice prior to the Confirmation ceremony, the diocesan examiner asked a young girl, "How many Gods are there?" The girl was thrown by this question. She blushed and was silent. Her mother, who was present, intervened at this point. "Excuse me now, Father", she said and turned to her daughter whom she had been preparing for this day. "Now listen", she said, "if all the Gods were at home in heaven to-day, how many would there be?" Her daughter replied happily, "One". In neither of these instances does the mystery of the Trinity make much impact on the children concerned. Mystery is indeed acknowledged but it is stillborn.

There is a world of difference between deciding to take a tour of Killarney or Connemara in one day and deciding simply to enjoy the beauty of those places. While the appeal and the mystery of a place of natural beauty may in some way be captured on film and brought home to be enjoyed later, the same is not true of the mystery of a person. A person, like a symphony, is to be appreciated, marvelled and wondered at. We do injustice to people when we think we have understood them, when we think we have 'captured' them. Persons are mysteries to be appreciated and contemplated, when they choose to reveal themselves. We can never exhaust the mystery of another person nor can anyone exhaust the mystery which each one of us is. When we approach the Divine Persons, this is all the more true. Unless They decide to reveal Themselves, we know very little about Them. When They do choose to reveal Themselves, the mystery springs into life and becomes a source of energy, joy and praise. It provokes an enthusiastic response. It is as if God has been slumbering within us and has suddenly woken up!

FROM MYSTERY TO MYSTERY

Ignatius of Loyola

About the year 1522, Ignatius of Loyola was praying at Manresa in Spain, on the steps of a monastery, when he experienced the most Holy Trinity under the symbol of three notes of a chord in harmony. This experience gave rise to uncontrollable tears. After dinner he could not talk about anything but the Holy Trinity. In trying to explain this afterwards, he made many different comparisons and was filled with great joy and consolation. This was how it was to be for the rest of his life. Here we have the same mystery, as in our earlier stories, but in this case the mystery brings a person forward, grabs hold of him and changes his life. Ignatius, at this moment, was not grappling with an insoluble mystery. He was experiencing a relationship with the Three Divine Persons which swept him off his feet and transformed everything in his life. We hope that something like this may happen to you even if in a milder, less dramatic way. What is important is that the relationship between the Three Divine Persons and yourself will grow and become central in your life, in your choices and in the way you see yourself and others.

Thou Hast Made Me Endless

In our previous booklet, *Reflective Living,* we spoke about the endless mystery which each one of us is. Each one of us carries more than a touch of divinity, because we are made in God's image and likeness. When searching for our deepest roots we find them in Him. A woman, seeing an unhappy neighbour coming up the street, said to her friend, "Here comes the sorrowful mysteries!" This remark was perhaps unkind but there is a point to it. Each of us is one of the mysteries of religion and, hopefully, we can be listed among the joyful and the glorious rather than the sorrowful ones. We all belong to God and, therefore, we are all worthy of infinite respect and reverence. Thomas Merton puts it like this: "Then it was as if I suddenly saw the secret beauty of their hearts, the depths of their hearts where neither sin nor desire nor self-knowledge can reach, the core of reality, the person that each one is in God's eyes. If only they could all see themselves as they really *are*. If only we could see each other that way all the time. There would be no more war, no more hatred, no more cruelty, no more greed . . . I suppose the big problem would be that we would fall down and worship each other". (*Conjectures of a Guilty Bystander,* p. 158.)

Electrons and Persons

A physicist will tell you that it takes many years of concentrated study to come to some understanding of electrons. Most people assume that it is easier to understand people than electrons; after all, unlike electrons, people are there before you, and you can see, hear and touch them. We can easily dismiss people as being unimportant. We see through them, or so we think. In doing so, we lose sight of the mystery of each person. If it takes many years to understand electrons, it takes even longer to come to an appreciation of human persons. Moreover, it takes a lifetime and eternity itself to come to a full appreciation of the Persons who are God. We need to put on our 'mystery boots' to explore the mystery of God. The place to begin is with ourselves. This brings us to the questions: Do we truly appreciate ourselves? Which of us spends enough time pondering, in awed wonder, on the fact that we are the images of God and so we are mysteries which mirror in some faint way the mystery that is God? Insofar as we do not appreciate ourselves, we lack true appreciation of others. We can only come to appreciate ourselves rightly if someone else appreciates us.

This booklet is an attempt to show you, the reader, just how much God appreciates you. As you grow in self-appreciation, you will be empowered to appreciate others truly. So the transformation of the world takes a step forward and the growth of the human community becomes enhanced. It is a startling, a joyous and also a disturbing fact to come to realise that both you and all those around you are mysteries in the most correct sense of that word. In a list of the mysteries of God, each man and woman's name must find an honoured and unique place. Each one of us is a wonderful mystery, a small echo of God and it is a gift of God to grasp this fact.

How They See You

The following quotations from the New Testament, chosen out of hundreds, illustrate the point that you are truly a mystery of God. Take them for prayerful pondering. Allow them space in your heart. Let them be with you when you work, take the bus, drive, walk alone, or share them with someone else who is engaged in the same quest as yourself: the quest of appreciating mystery.

"The Father has called you to eternal glory in Christ" (I Peter 5:10).
"You will be revealed in all your glory with Christ" (Col. 3:4).
"You have the spirit of glory, the spirit of God resting on you" (I Peter 4:14).

In these texts, we meet the Trinity. Each person is mentioned twice, since the word 'God' in the last text refers, as so often in the New Testament, to the Father. The three quotations use the word 'glory', which means 'importance', and is an attribute of God. In our three quotations, we see that the glory which is proper to God belongs also in some mysterious way to us; not only after our death but even in our present situation no matter what it may be. So, if we have to choose between calling ourselves joyful, sorrowful or glorious mysteries, these three golden texts give us ground for asserting that each of us is a glorious mystery of God. This is one of the hardest 'lessons' to learn but all we can do is try to be open to it.

"We're all VIPs!"

Statements like the three above abound in Scripture and are inexhaustible

16

in their richness. One aspect of this richness is that while they refer to each one of us uniquely, they refer also to the people around us. A married woman, who undertook the experiment of praying over these statements of God about herself, remarked after some time: "It's changing my life to realise that God thinks that I'm glorious! It's hard to believe with my life in a mess, but it's great too! It's very challenging to know that He thinks that way about other people, especially the ones I find boring or difficult. So I've had to change my attitude towards them. I'm also becoming more hopeful in my heart. The state of the world used to get me down a lot. I'd become depressed. Now I know, in a dim way, that He thinks the world of everyone. There's hope for us all, no matter what happens".

The Mystery of Love

We are concerned here with a mystery which, when we enter into it, fascinates us and draws us upwards, onwards and beyond ourselves. Insofar as we experience the love of another, we have a deep experience or awareness of mystery. To experience true love is to be drawn into endless mystery. St Paul says, when speaking about love: "It does not come to an end; it is endless, as we are" (I Cor. 13). Love makes us wake up to the mystery of ourselves. It makes us rejoice in being who we are and it calls forth in us responding love. Mystery and love are intimately bound together.

Love, like mystery, is not to be explained away but to be rejoiced in. It is to be accepted reverently, as a pure gift. We become loving people only by being loved first. If a child experiences the love of its parents, it grows and becomes a full person. The love of its parents creates its personality. Each of us, no matter what our personal history, can remember instances of being loved by others and it is a worthwhile exercise to note some of these. As we grow to notice them sensitively, we grow in gratitude and in responding love. So we become generative of love. We are free to take a more loving initiative with others. Love is mysterious. There is no explaining it away, no ultimate reason lies behind it.

The love, for example, of parents for a handicapped child illustrates the point. The parents just love the child but will probably not be able to explain why. The love that is shown in forgiveness also bears this out, as when, perhaps, in the North of Ireland a family forgives those who have murdered one of their relatives. The mystery of love in the world has its origin beyond the world. As the poet, T.S. Eliot, put it, it has its origins at "the still point of the turning world". According as we reflect on the mystery of love in our lives, we are drawn into the mystery of God.

God is totally good and loving but our sins bring a warp into a good creation. There is the problem of evil to which there is no human solution. God is good and He cares, and so there is a *divine* solution to it. God holds steadfast in the face of evil and, wherever we find love holding steadfast against evil in our world or in our own lives, we find ourselves facing a mystery. That mystery is an intimation of God's love which never wavers nor is ever put off by evil.

Hidden Treasure

Let us give one example. The Russian author, Solzhenitsyn, tells the story of an old woman, Matryona, whose rapacious relations were grabbing her few last possessions. She was the kind of person who was always helping others. Knowing that her relatives were dismantling part of her home to build a hut elsewhere, she helped them. When a load of wood broke loose from the tractor, which was dragging it across the railway line, they were hit by an engine and she was killed. "Misunderstood and rejected by her husband, a stranger to her own family despite her happy, amiable and comical temperament, so foolish that she worked for others for no reward, this woman, who had buried all her six children, had stored up no earthly goods. Nothing but a dirty white goat, a lame cat and a row of fig plants. We all lived beside her and did not understand that she was a just person without whom, according to the proverb, the village could not endure. Nor the city. Nor all our land". ("Matryona's Home", in *Stories and Prose Poems*, p. 46).

Here we have an example of pure love; love shining out through the tattiness of human selfishness, shining like a light which will not be quenched. There is no explaining the mystery of this love. It is to be contemplated, respected and imitated. Such love would and does transform our darkened lives. Such love is an expression of God's love.

Jean Vanier, founder of the L'Arche Communities, keeps telling us that people in misery do not need a look that judges and criticises. They need a strengthening presence that brings peace, hope and life whether by word or by body-language or by some small kindness done. These people in misery must be shown that they are human beings, important, mysterious and infinitely precious. We each need to know from others that in us there are those seeds of the infinite which must rise from the earth of our misery so that humanity may be complete.

Try for yourself the experiment of going back over to-day, then yesterday and perhaps the day before, until you come to an incident which, when you think about it now, strikes you as mysterious because of the love involved. Some of the essential elements which you may find will be the following: the love will involve another person or other persons, for true love is outgoing to others. Next, in the loving person there will be found the quality of openness or receptiveness; the person has space for another.

You may also find that loving people are at home with themselves. Consciously, or perhaps unconsciously, such people accept themselves and have reverence for themselves. They have found themselves; as a result they are free. They are not preoccupied any longer with the task of finding themselves, with searching for personal pearls of great price. Instead, their freedom allows them to help others find *their* pearls of great price. Putting it another way, loving people are happy to some degree at least, with the song which is their life. Thus they come to know in some way that others have a song to sing, the song of their life. They are happy to help others to find the words of that song. God is like that. The Three Divine Persons are each at home with

Themselves, happy about Themselves, totally receptive of each other. So They sing a song, They sing one song. Their joy now is to help all of us to learn our song and to sing it well, the hidden pearl song of humanity.

Conchita

We might say that loving people are a kind of Noah's Ark to others in need, to those who feel that they are in danger of drowning. Take this example: Conchita began receiving strange phone calls, mostly in the mornings. Sometimes she would have as many as thirty calls in one morning but each time she lifted the receiver, no one answered. She was aware that someone was at the other end, keeping silent. Conchita kept in her mind that whoever was at the other end, was a person who was probably seeking someone or something. After a number of days, she received a letter from a girl named Christina. She wrote saying that when she was alone at home she'd take the telephone directory and dial a number, any number. The letter read, "With your number, someone answered so immediately afterwards I phoned again. I felt something in my heart. So I began to phone you over and over, just to hear someone say, "Yes. Who are you?", then that gentle replacing of the receiver. It seemed to me that after I made these calls my day would go better. The first time I phoned you was very important for me because you didn't make a fool of me like my friends do. I'm a drug addict and that particular day I was going to give myself an injection. I didn't, because — as I said — I felt something in my heart".

The next time Conchita received a call, she thanked Christina for the letter and tried to encourage her to say something. Finally, a far-away voice reached her, a thread of a voice saying "Yes". Then, timidly, Christina began to whisper, almost against her will, with silent pauses, then taking courage again. Over a long period, Christina sang the song of her life, a sad song, but Conchita received it well. After some time, Christina was able to accept it and become a loving person herself.

God is like that: He listens with infinite reverence. He has infinite space for us to speak our story and make it into a song. This is the mystery of love in the world, the mystery that begins and has its source and will have its end in the love of God.

GRACE: THE MYSTERIOUS TOUCH OF GOD'S LOVE

In speaking about grace we come to the heart of the mystery of God because grace is all about relationships, all about good relationships between persons. Perhaps, instead of using the word 'grace', it would be better if we spoke of 'graced relationships'. For all the evil and misery that spoil the pages of human history, there is yet something wonderful astir in our world. With the coming of Christ a new community of persons, bonded together by graced relationships, began to emerge in our world. At the heart of this new community stood the Three Divine Persons who called each and every one of us to join Them in Their Divine Life of joy and happiness. The transformation of human history began

19

here. The world into which these graced relationships emerged, was a world in disgrace, a world disfigured and warped by evil, sin and death. It was into this disgraced world, this chaotic and messy world, that the Son of God came. He gathered disciples, He revealed to them His Father's love and His Father's plan for them. He shared with them His own spirit. His one command in this new community was that those who were gathered into it should love one another and should relate in a graced way to each other. The model of their love was to be that of Jesus Himself, who showed an unlimited love which was forgiving, which was costly, which remained steadfast in the face of rejection and disloyalty. Jesus founded the final community of love, whose visible expression was the Christian community, light for a darkened world. In the Church, He gave it all the needed means of growth: the Word and the Sacraments and the support of community.

This community will be perfected at the end of time. What began so small, with Jesus gathering the disciples in Galilee nearly 2,000 years ago, will then be seen fully grown. All humankind, we may hope, will be gathered at the feast of the Three Divine Persons. The ebb and flow of human history, much of it so meaningless to us, will then be seen to have a meaning. What is really happening is that through the incredibly tangled web of events and through all the sorrow and the tears, God has brought about the final community of love.

Grace is Everywhere

The world of grace, of graced relationships, can best be understood in terms of friendship. This friendship is universal. The reverence which Jesus showed to those around Him, to His disciples and even to His enemies, is to be the model of our reverence for all others. Only at the end of time will friendship be perfected in this way. Even now, however, we touch on the deepest mystery of God whenever we find ourselves reverenced, accepted totally, rejoiced over, delighted in, important — V.I.P.s

Insofar as we recognize another person as a beloved son or daughter of God, we are touching on the deepest mystery of the universe. When we pray for others, as parents do for their children, or as some people do in an empty church for those who most need their prayers or when we sit silently on our own and give time and space to God to allow His mystery to settle more deeply in our hearts, then we are sharing in the transformation of the world. When we pray for the world that it may "grow in love" (*Eucharistic Prayer II*), we are praying for the completion of the Body of Christ.

When we contemplate Jesus in the New Testament in order to become like Him, we are playing our part in developing the mystery of graced relationships in our world. When we struggle to forgive those who have wronged us, we are building the bridges of spoiled relationships and are contributing to the final community.

Although we do not see it now, no loving deed, prayer or wish of ours for others is wasted but will come to flower in its own time. All else that is not love will fade away but love is eternal. It does not fade. When we struggle in our lives

20

to make space for God, to allow Him to be Lord for us, we are redeeming our own human history and also the history of those among whom we live. Only at the end will we see perhaps the part we have played in the bringing forward of God's plan. We will see that we helped, often without being aware, often without knowing how, often almost in spite of ourselves. We will see that when it was most costly, painful, draining, demanding, that then it was most worthwhile.

When we gather as a Christian community at the parish Mass on Sunday, we may often feel little or nothing. We may have many negative feelings such as thinking the liturgy boring or badly prepared. We sometimes have our own problems to contend with and may be struggling to accept some of the other people who are there. At the end, we will see that these ordinary, humdrum liturgies with all their human inadequacies were high points in which the community put God first and showed that it accepted His invitation to join Him at His table. When we are in pain, lying ill perhaps for many days or months or years, when we are close to death, we often find that we cannot pray. Yet grace shines out here in our weakness, in our resignation, in allowing God to hollow us out so that He may fill us with Himself. In these and in countless other ways we can come to notice more and more the mystery of God as it plays around us. We can notice how, as the years pass, we come to accept God more, to rely on Him more. We want to become better people, in the face of our weakness and our sinfulness. We are surrounded by the mystery of grace. As the dying curate says at the end of George Bernanos' *The Diary of a Country Priest,* when no one could in time come to give him the last rites, "grace is everywhere".

"Take off Your Shoes" (Exodus 3:5)

As we begin to grasp the mystery of grace, so ordinary in its manifestations and yet so profound, we come to understand the mystery of God and His ceaseless working in our lives. For human history is graced history, with its dark side all too obvious to us but with its light side there also if we look for it. Wherever we find someone standing for truth, for justice, for peace, for the good of others, there we find grace. The more we reflect on our lives and notice what is going on in them, the more the mystery of grace shines out in them.

Margaret Hebblethwaite remarks, in *Finding God in All Things,* that when we look carefully over a period of empty prayer, we may find, more often than we had realised, little insights here and soft shadows there of the love of God — slight graces, half hidden. Often, graces are like that. They are not like great dramatic bangs that leave us with no doubt of God's presence but more like little brush strokes that need to be taken together before the picture is slowly built up. Grace, she adds, may not be noticed at all, unless we have accustomed ourselves to looking for its almost imperceptible action.

We must then, like Mary, store all the events of our lives in our hearts. We must ponder them, treasure them, gradually learn to appreciate the presence of God in them and so walk in a world that is full of meaning, a world which is full of love.

God is indeed more difficult to understand than electrons but He is easy to appreciate. All we need to do is recapture that sense of wonder that we each had as children and apply it to the mystery of our world, of our lives, of our destiny. When you appreciate any creature, you are moving towards an appreciation of the God who made it. In looking for God, it is good to look at small things because perhaps we can manage them better. G.K. Chesterton said, "I'm glad to be alive for the privilege of looking at a dandelion". Or as Tagore, the Indian poet, put it, "God grows weary of great kingdoms but never of little flowers".

The Mystery of God in Human Form

The central point of this booklet is that God is not distant and remote: He is very close to us. What can prevent us from noticing this is that we could be looking for God in one form but fail to find Him there. We need to be open to whatever form God chooses to reveal Himself. We have touched on the mysteries of nature which reveal traces of God, His footprints as it were. "Creation is the monstrance of God", said Hans Urs von Balthasar. We, as Christians, appreciate the presence of God in Scripture and in the Sacraments: those symbols in which He touches us directly and in which we meet Him intimately.

In recent years, perhaps we are coming more and more to appreciate God in human form. The mystery of the Incarnation is not seen simply as the presence of God in one individual man, Jesus, but the presence of God in every person. The Incarnation of God is in the whole of humanity. This is God's preferred way of revealing Himself, it seems. We are meant to reveal the face of God, the heart of God, the care of God to one another. People will have a right appreciation of God only if we reveal Him correctly to them. This is obvious in the case of children but is also true for grown-ups. People desperately need to have a clear vision of Him and it is up to each one of us to reveal God rightly to those around us. A child, asked by his mother what he was drawing, replied, "I'm drawing a picture of God". His mother objected. "But you can't do that because no one knows what God looks like". "They will know when I've finished", replied the child. This can be true of each of us. We can tell others what God is like when we've finished sketching — and, hopefully, long before we've finished sketching — the picture of our own lives. By the way we show love, or the way we do not show love, we either reveal God or obscure and eclipse Him. A young woman told her story to a social worker: "My husband beats me up. I'm eighteen and have two children already. He doesn't love me. I've nothing and we've nothing. How can you say God cares?" The social worker put down her pen and said: "I can't. I can tell you only that I care". In this brief encounter God was present. God revealed Himself through the caring social worker. In her love, God's love was present. Was this obvious to the young wife? We can only hope that it was, that someone might have shown her that this was the way God chose to reveal Himself: in His care and in His compassion. If she recognised this, she would have realised that there would be many similar instances throughout her life where she would find God. She would have realised that God is not distant but is as close to us as other people can be.

A priest lay on his hospital bed, in constant pain. His leg ached day and night. The nights were the worst because he could not sleep for the pain and discomfort. There was a Crucifix on the wall opposite him and he used to fix his eyes on it and pray to Jesus on the Cross, saying, "God have mercy on me and ease my pain. Let me sleep a little". But God seemed asleep or uncaring. The figure on the Cross was mute and unmoving. Anger would well up in the priest. No God came. Others came: the night nurse, with cups of tea to while away the hours of darkness and of pain. Next came the old man with the papers and the funny remarks. Then the wardsmaid with breakfast. Then nursing staff and doctors; then the physiotherapist, the other patients, visitors and the priest on his daily round, giving Holy Communion.

Slowly, he learnt the lesson which God was trying to teach him. Truly the figure on the Crucifix had not spoken nor moved a hand or a muscle. But God *had* come and comforted him and strengthened him and healed him through all these people with their simple gestures of kindness and love. He came to see that God has not two hands but an almost infinite number of hands: the hands of all those in the world who care. Father Peter Lemass, the Dublin priest who died in early 1988 of a brain tumour while only in middle years, spoke of the hands that held him which later he came to see as the hands of God. The hands of doctors and surgeons working expertly on his brain; the hands of nurses and orderlies; the hands of fellow priests laid on him in blessing and absolution; the hands of friends who came to visit him; the hand of the Eucharistic minister; the safe hands of ambulance-drivers and stretcher-bearers. These he came to see as the hands of God multiplied and available.

The Hands of God

In *The Divine Milieu,* Teilhard de Chardin speaks of the two hands of God: one which holds us with infinite care and the other which moulds the world where each one of us has a place, a place He is preparing for us. The mystery which we must grasp, if we are to find God is that God works through all hands: from the hands of the nurse or doctor who bring us as babies into this world, to the hands of those who prepare us for burial. God is present behind them all, through them all and it is in this way that he is so intimate with us. If we fail to recognise His presence in these ways, we have an impoverished relationship with God. On the other hand, when we see God in others, we are able to rejoice in God's Incarnation in human persons whenever they show love. This helps us to realise that we, too, are called to make God present in our own place and time to those around us. Perhaps God could have done it all alone; certainly He could. Take the example of a family who are going to have a large celebration. The parents in charge of operations have a choice. They may say to the children in the morning: "Everybody out, now. No one is to come into the kitchen until we have everything ready". Or they may say at the breakfast table: "We're all in this together. We want everyone to play their part. Now, everyone into the kitchen and we'll show you what to do". Perhaps if the parents decide to work on their own, the work will be done on time and will be much applauded by the rest of the family. They will surely be exhausted, however, and the family will feel perhaps a little guilty that they did nothing to help. Maybe they will even feel resentful because they could not exercise whatever talents they had in the culinary field. On the contrary, if the parents involve everyone in the kitchen, there will certainly be some disasters. Someone will spill the cream on the floor. Someone else will burn the meat or the meal will be ready a little late. Perhaps there will be some rows and some tears. At the end, if the parents manage to co-ordinate their troops, they will all experience the joy of having played their part in the final outcome.

God has chosen the second alternative in His planning of the cosmic party with which human history will terminate. In choosing this way, He knows that many things will go wrong, that there will be many tears and many mistakes. This is His preferred way. As Jesus says in St John's Gospel, "Sower and reaper will rejoice together" (4:36). We will rejoice with God because of the part we have played in the final outcome of human history, in the formation of the final community of love.

SITTING AT THEIR TABLE

In this booklet we have been exploring various aspects of mystery; golden threads that lead us towards the mystery behind all other mysteries.

Our questions now can be phrased thus: What is God like? Do you have any experience of Him? How can you come to appreciate Him? If someone asked you these questions, perhaps it would help if you asked in turn: Have you ever met genuine, human sympathy and understanding? Do you have experience of gentleness and concern, of a person's attention and affection being fully focussed on you? If the reply is "Yes", then you could say: God is like that.

To illustrate, let us take Chesterton's description of the way in which Saint Francis of Assisi related to the people he met. Francis, according to Chesterton, saw in people the image of God 'multiplied but not monotonous'. To him, a person was always a person who did not disappear in a dense crowd and become merely a number. Francis honoured all people: He not only loved but respected them all and this gave him his extraordinary personal power. People who looked into those brown, burning eyes were certain that their owner was really interested in their inner life from the cradle to the grave; they were certain that they were being valued and taken seriously.

God is like that. Just as Saint Francis saw in everyone the image of God, 'multiplied but not monotonous', so God attends to each and every one of us with the immensity of divine, gentle attention. Francis' genuine, human sympathy and understanding, his gentleness and concern, his attention and affection are an indication of the sympathy and understanding, the gentleness and concern, the attention and affection of God. God attends to you and me in that way. God sees to the heart. There, at our innermost, is where our true face is to be found. There is where gold glitters; there the hidden pearl lies; there gleams the image and likeness of God.

A good marriage grows over the years through mutual attention of the man and woman towards each other, expressed in a myriad of ways. Appreciation of one partner grows through the serious love shown by the other. Scripture uses the rich imagery of the marriage relationship to illustrate the relationship between God and ourselves. From quiet beginnings, this relationship should develop over the years, with all the nuances of joy and appreciation that come in married life, through the sharing of all events, both happy and sad, painful and delightful. A good marriage involves a sharing of interests and values.

In our relationship with God there is no lack of attention on God's part towards us, not even for an instant. God is totally present, attentive to you even as you read these words. If the relationship between God and ourselves languishes and dries up, it is not because God has lost interest or lacks attention. It is we who lack attention. "Attention to what?", you may ask. Attention to the mystery of all things and all persons. The sort of attention that Saint Francis of Assisi had for the gestures of God in nature, in persons and in all the events that touched his life.

We need, then, to grow in attentiveness, to grow in reflectiveness. We need to untie our childlike sense of wonder and let it grow to an appreciation of the meaning and the mystery of our world and of our lives and also to the mystery of our destiny. Our destiny lies not in a place nor in a situation but in a group of Persons.

As we write, we do not pretend to understand everything about God and His world but we are open to being drawn more fully into the mystery of it all as the situations of life unfold from day to day.

It is time now to turn from the image which Saint Francis gave us in the 13th century to another one: the Rublev Icon of the 15th century. For five hundred years this visual image has profoundly helped people in their appreciation of God.

The Rublev Icon

In 1425, Andrew Rublev painted his icon of the Holy Trinity in memory of a great Russian, Saint Sergius (1313-1392). Rublev was a monk who wanted to bring the people of Russia together by their contemplation of the Holy Trinity. His icon was the fruit of his own deep contemplation of the mystery of the Holy Trinity. By contemplating the icon, we will also be drawn into a deeper appreciation of the mystery of God.

There are innumerable commentaries on this icon. All we will do, in this booklet, is make some brief remarks about various aspects of it, insofar as it illuminates the mystery of God, the mystery of the Trinity. If you, the reader, wish to explore the details of the icon further, you can turn to books such as Henri Nouwen's *Behold the Beauty of the Lord: Praying with Icons.*

The Space at the Table

In the icon, the Three Divine Persons are depicted as three visitors who are wearing travellers' clothes. They have staffs in Their hands, sandals on Their feet and They have their cloaks draped over one shoulder. They have come a long distance and will soon move on again. They are winged. The painting is based on an episode in Genesis (18:1-5), where Abraham welcomes three travellers and then stands beside them as they eat the meat which his wife, Sarah, has prepared for them. A title given to the icon is 'The Welcome that makes a Stranger into a Friend'. There is an open space at one side of the table. It is an invitation to each of us, to all of us, to take our place at Their table and to share Their meal and Their life.

There is much revealed to us here about the mystery of the Trinity. The life of God, the life of the Trinity can only be understood in terms of relationships, loving relationships. They relate to each other in perfect love. They are in perfect sympathy and understanding with one another. They are full of gentleness and concern, of attention and affection, each for the others. This perfection of relationship, of openness to each other is not restricted to Themselves. They are not closed in on Themselves, careless of humanity. We are not asked to contemplate Them at a distance, as it were, admiring Them but feeling that we are outsiders. We are not like the man, Lazarus, in Saint Luke's

26

Gospel, who lay at the gate of the rich man's house, gazing longingly at the feasts which the rich man enjoyed but finding that there was no invitation for him to join them. No, it is not like that. It is rather the opposite.

The icon stresses the open place that is reserved for you and for me at Their table. The space speaks of hospitality, of invitation, of readiness to give Themselves and of welcome. So the life of the Trinity is all about relationships, Theirs with one another and with us. In Their relationship with you, They encompass all you could ever want of love, acceptance, complete appreciation, unending support and encouragement. They are the fulfillment of all you could yearn for. You are invited, then, into Their company, the best of company; to move within Their circle and to come to know the best friends you can ever have.

God Within and Without

Can you truly talk about Their life and your life in one breath, as it were? Where do They and you meet? Where is the table in reality? Saint Paul speaks of the mystery of God as surrounding us: "It is in God that we live and move and have our being" (Acts 17:27). The table in this sense is all around us. Teilhard de Chardin called his autobiography *The Divine Milieu,* inferring that God is the surrounding atmosphere of our lives. You can rightly think then of God as surrounding you, as enfolding you in sympathy and understanding and care and love. You can also think of the table as being set in your own heart, at the deepest level of your being. The Three Divine Persons and yourself meet within your heart, within you. The term given for this aspect of the presence of God is 'immanence'. 'Immanence' means 'to remain within, to dwell within'. The indwelling of Father, Son and Holy Spirit in our hearts is explored fully and wonderfully in Saint John's Gospel (chapters 14 to 17). The table is within. They are there, at the deepest point of your being and They invite you within. God without, God within: there is no limiting the mystery of the closeness of the Three Divine Persons to us, of Their presence to the most intimate details of our lives. Let Them become the atmosphere in which you live your life.

Take your Place

Before going on, spend some little time imagining the Three Divine Persons as present both outside you and then inside you. Savour the mystery. Reflect on your experience of being at table with other people. Go back to your childhood and recall being at the family table with your father and mother, brothers and sisters. Perhaps you can remember the first time you were let sit at the table when there were visitors. Think of what that meant to you, especially if you liked the visitors. To be sent away from the table then would have been heart-breaking. Think of meals that you have shared with close friends, or one particular friend, and savour the quality of the presence of one person to the other. Think of meals which you wished might never end, not that you wanted more to eat or drink, but that you wanted the quality of presence, of attentive and gentle love, to go on. To be at the table then was to be at ease, to be content, to be satisfied. There was a joy in knowing the other person and being known oneself. There was sharing of what was most important, of values and views and experiences. You were yourself and you allowed the other person or persons to be themselves.

Such images give you a hint of what it means to be at Their table. It is over to you to stay at Their table, to experience this sense of being at home, to experience the ease and contentment in sharing and receiving. The more time you give to this the more you are drawn into love and appreciation of who They are, what kind They are and how They think of you. The destiny of your life and every person's life is to be in Their company, to move within Their circle, to come to know Them as best friends. They are the best of company. Our hearts are made to know Them, our lives are meant to be unendingly enriched by Their love and friendship. Think of what good company, good friendship means to you. By doing this, human experience points you to the Eternal, to divine friends and company.

At this table we experience welcome and hospitality. We are given a welcome which makes us into friends of Theirs. The invitation is permanent on Their side, the space at the table is always there. The table of the Eucharist is a permanent reminder of the readiness of the Three Divine Persons to receive us. There They wash our feet, chat with us about Themselves, make us feel at home, prepare a meal for us and share with us Their life, Their vision and Their love. From our side we need to provide the space in our hearts where They can come and have Their meal and be at home. From this point of view we are like Abraham; we are the hosts and They the Guests. We need to offer Them the welcome that makes a stranger into a friend. They want to be received into our hearts, into our lives. "Look, I am standing at the door, knocking. If one of you hears me calling and opens the door, I will come in to share your meal, side by side with you" (Rev. 3:20).

We must then keep both aspects of the table in mind: the table to which They invite us and the table to which we invite Them. While this may seem a little complicated, it is the way things are in human life, for we are welcomed to the tables of others, into their homes and hearts and in turn we welcome others to our table, into our homes and into our hearts. Relationships cannot be one-sided. There is receiving and there is sharing and giving.

Their Company

As we meet Them at Their table or in our hearts, we come to know some aspects of Their company. The main characteristic which shines out for us is Their unconditional and total love for us. Julian of Norwich, the 14th century English mystic, wrote of the homeliness, the courtesy, the graciousness of the Trinity. She wrote of Their enfolding of us. By staying at the table of the Trinity, we allow Them to enfold us. This is, of course, what They are always doing but according as we allow Them to enfold us willingly and make ourselves available for that, our lives are changed and our happiness grows. More and more we come to recognise Them in the events of our lives and in the persons whom we encounter and in the mystery of our own selves.

Developing relationships can be a risk and calls for trust. So how can we be sure of them? Will we be respected, especially when we reveal something of ourselves which we do not like? Will They be interested? In befriending the Three Divine Persons we need not be afraid of what this may involve. They are to be trusted fully and we can come close to Them and feel safe in Their company because They are love, love which is to be trusted without any reservation. For us it takes a long time to trust fully. That is because we are fragile and vulnerable, and are easily hurt. The more we trust ourselves to another, as in friendship and marriage, the more exposed and vulnerable we become and if our love is betrayed we are deeply wounded. This is because of the warp in humanity of which we spoke before.

However, the Three Divine Persons are outside that warp, They are not caught in it. We must allow these Three guests of ours to be Themselves. We must not colour our view of Them because of the darkness that colours some of our human relationships, even relationships with persons who are very close to us, like our parents. For even those closest to us are caught in the warp and, without intending to do so, they can spoil our lives to some degree even in their efforts to love us rightly.

So it is all right to be at the beginning stage of trusting the Three Divine Persons but we must intend moving forward. They are totally to be trusted. They trust us totally. They open up Their lives to us and become vulnerable. The Son entrusted Himself totally to humanity. His trust in humanity was betrayed but not His trust in His Father. His trust was vindicated in His resurrection. We, therefore, must keep our eyes on the Son, so that we will grow in trust, and move more and more fully into Their circle with confidence and peace of heart. The invitation to this relationship remains open always for us to accept it more fully.

What do They say to Each Other?

In the icon we see the Three Persons faced towards one another. The usual interpretation is that the Father is on the left, the Son in the centre and the Spirit on the right-hand side. The Son and the Spirit are leaning towards the Father, hearing Him reverently and responding to Him. They are in conversation and They have been in conversation from the beginning. Theirs is a conversation in the Eternal Now. Their conversation is on two levels: They speak about Themselves and They also speak of us. What do they say to one another? As good conversation among people involves sharing, being received, understood and accepted, among the Three Divine Persons, the conversation is perfect, each person expressing Himself fully and being fully received by the others. Each knows the others and is fully known by Them. Each loves the others and is fully loved in return.

In the New Testament the Son is called 'the Word'. When we speak, we try to communicate what is in our minds and hearts and we use words. We can think of when the Father was deciding to express fully what was in His mind and His heart. Being God, He expressed Himself totally and completely in one word, *the* Word. The Son was the full expression of what the Father wanted to say. We can identify with this when we reflect on a good conversation and say to ourselves "I've said all I wanted to say". In this situation we are content. We are at peace and we experience joy. If we think about it, we can recognise that we love what we have said because what we have spoken is the truth. It is similar with the Three Divine Persons. The Father spoke Himself fully and the word that was spoken was the Son. The Father was content with what He had spoken and He loved what He had said and this love was the Holy Spirit. The difference between our speaking and loving and Theirs, is that while we labour to express the truth fully, we only do so partially, because we are creatures.

So we catch a mere glimpse, but a very precious glimpse, of the mystery of the Three Divine Persons and what Their conversation is about by noticing what goes on in our own conversation as we express the truth in words, and love the truth which we have spoken.

To give an analogy, imagine an artist labouring to express, on canvas, in stone, or in bronze, some great vision of truth and beauty that is in her mind and heart. She succeeds. Her work has satisfied her desire and she stands back and gazes on it. She loves it. It is how she wanted it to be. Here again we have an image of how things are among the Trinity. There is the expression of the truth, the communication of it and the love of it. A great sculptor can express a creative idea and we see the finished statue of a person. This statue is lifeless but we can imagine that if God were the sculptor he could have created a statue that would be alive. We think of Michelangelo's command to the statue of David when he had just finished it. He stood back and cried out: "Speak!". Of course, there was no answer. With God, however, the Father succeeded where the artist failed. The Word lived. The Word expressed the Father fully. The Father was delighted with the Son: this was the delight of love.

Here is another image. A married couple express their love for one another in mutual self-giving and the fruit of their love is a child. In the child the parents see something of themselves. They love the child they see. So the pattern is the same: from creativity, to expression, to love of what is expressed.

Such reflections can open our eyes to what goes on between the Three Divine Persons. In Their conversation, each is totally open to the others, each expresses the others fully, each delights totally in the others. The Father delights in the Son and the Son delights in the Father. The Holy Spirit is the personal expression of the total love between Father and Son. We shall return to Their inter-relationships later.

They're Talking about Us

We mentioned earlier that there is another level to the conversation between the Three Persons in the icon: They are speaking about us. We are Their concern, just as in the Genesis story the whole point of the visit of the three strangers was to tell Abraham and Sarah that they would have a child. In the icon, the Son is responding to the Father. He is saying His eternal 'Yes' to the desire which the Father has shared with Him about the salvation of humankind. "The Father so loved the world that He wished to send His Son so that those who believed in Him would not perish but have eternal life" (John 3:16). The Son is saying: "Behold I come to do your will, my Father" (Heb. 10:7). The conversation continues even as you read. The conversation underlies all our history, it is at the centre of the wheel of time.

We are the focus of a divine conspiracy of love. That is the essence of Their conversation. We may call that conversation 'prayer' because that is what it is. In prayer, the Father speaks and we come to know what is on His mind and in His heart for us, whether through our pondering on Scripture or in silent contemplation. The Son shows the proper response to the love of the Father. The response is 'Yes', the 'Yes' of a loving surrender. That is the heart of prayer from our point of view. It is the 'amen' which we are meant to utter; a glad and joyous response to the goodness of God. Their conversation takes place at the heart of things, "at the still point of the turning world". It takes place, it finds its echo in our hearts, if we stop and listen.

Your heart is the place where They wish to pray now. Prayer has already begun in you because of Their conversation with one another in your heart. As you read, we hope that you will be able to attend to Their conversation, that you will be able to hear the Father and that you will be able to respond as the Son responded. The Son is always talking to the Father about you, and the Holy Spirit is always praying in you, even when you do not know it. The music, the eternal and perfect music, plays about you and resonates in your heart. You can become more and more aware of it and, as you learn it, you can join in and add your voice to the voice of the Son speaking to the Father in the love of the Holy Spirit.

We are like children sitting at the table with our parents. As children, we understand little of what they are saying. As time goes by, however, we catch on and we join in the conversation, sometimes well and sometimes poorly. Our parents, if they are loving, accept our efforts, our stumbling and our stammering. They know that, given time and love, we will learn to respond fully and to play a better part in the conversation.

This may offer a suitable background for what Saint Paul means when he speaks of the Spirit coming to help us in our weakness. When we cannot choose our words in order to pray properly, the Spirit Himself expresses our plea in a way that could never be put into words. Thus the Father, who knows everything in our hearts, knows perfectly well what we mean. The plea cannot be put into words because our desire goes beyond words, just as the Son's desire goes beyond words. It expresses itself fully only in action, in total self donation of life, in total openness to the Father.

Watching the Son with the Father

In coming to know one of the Persons, we grow in knowledge of the others because each one is always revealing the others and pointing to Them. In the icon, the Father's head is slightly inclined towards the Son who is in the centre.

The Father delights in the Son. He speaks to Him: "You are my beloved Son: in You I am well pleased. You are all my joy". The Father's hand is turned towards the Son in all tenderness. The parable of the Prodigal Son, which Jesus told, gives an image of the Father's love. In the parable, the father was watching out for his son. When he saw him, he ran to him, held him in his arms and kissed him tenderly. Then he showered him with every gift he had.

We must not think of the Father as being remote, cold, inaccessible, unmoved by the emotions which move us. Through the relationship of Father and Son as expressed in the Gospels, we can come to a deep love and appreciation and joy in regard to the Father. Although He remains very mysterious to us, in that we do not see Him directly, we can come to know Him and to love Him in the depths of our being and fully to Him as the Son did. It is mainly through the Son that we come to know the family life of the Trinity.

As children we may have brought one of our school friends home and introduced him or her to our parents and our brothers and sisters. This is similar to what Jesus did. Jesus came to tell us about His Father, to reveal Him to us. "No one knows my Father except myself, just as no one knows me as well as my Father does" (Matthew 11:27). The Son chose to reveal the Father to us. This was His mission. It is not enough to say that the mission of Jesus in the world was to save it, that would be to impoverish the truth. For many people, Christianity means relationship to the Son, Jesus. What Jesus wished was not only that we be related to Him but to His Father. His life was an attempt to reveal the heart of the Father to us and to show us how to respond to Him. This is what was most on His mind and in His heart. The Son only wanted to reveal to us who God is and who He is for us. So Jesus revealed that God is not one person acting alone but Three Persons acting in perfect communion and harmony.

He showed us what the Father thinks of us, the Father's infinite and inexhaustible love for us. He showed us the Father's intentions in our regard; He knows what we human beings are like, in all our magnificence and our misery. Jesus revealed what we are to be: His own brothers and sisters sharing with Him in the family life and joy of the Three Divine Persons.

In this section, we will keep our eyes "fixed on Jesus" (Heb. 12:2). We fix our eyes on "the one who is closest to the Father's heart and who has made Him known" (cf. John 1:18). During His life on earth, Jesus did not try to explain the Mystery of the Trinity. Instead He introduced people to His Father and He gave them Himself.

All Space for the Father

Jesus must have been disappointed, during the Last Supper, to hear Philip say, "Lord, let us see the Father and then we shall be satisfied". His reply was: "Have I been with you all this time, Philip, and you still do not know me? To have seen me is to have seen the Father" (John 14:8-9). In the icon, we see the Son in the centre, His face turned towards the Father. He seems carried away, fascinated, as He leans towards the Father. We are reminded of the attitude of Mary in Fra Angelico's *Annunciation*. She leans towards the angel, in total attentiveness and receptiveness. She is completely available to what the angel may ask of her. So it is with the Son in the icon. He is watching the Father, and all He wants to do is please Him (John 8:29). So there is perfect harmony in Their relationship. The Father is totally sure of the Son. The Father knows that the Son will never disappoint Him; rather there is a sense in which the Father's expectations of the Son are fulfilled in an overflowing way all the time.

We know the experience of waiting for someone whom we haven't seen for a long time. There is expectation and excitement in our hearts. When the person appears, the joy of the meeting goes far beyond the expectation in the waiting. Jesus knows that the Father delights in Him, that He finds all His joy in Him. And Jesus is happy in this. Reflect on how you feel when someone pays you a compliment. Is it easy to accept it and rest in it? Usually not. We see that Jesus is able to take a compliment and it is the eternal compliment. It lasts forever and it is mutual between the Persons. "You shall be called my delight" (Isaiah 62:4). Jesus is glad to delight His Father.

When you love someone very much, and they ask something of you, you delight in being able to grant it. Lovers want to do everything they can to please their beloveds. In his *Spiritual Exercises,* Saint Ignatius says that love consists in a mutual sharing of goods. For example, lovers both give and share what they possess. One is always giving to the other (*Spiritual Exercises,* n. 231). In the icon, we see that the Son wishes to fulfill the desire of the Father about the salvation of humankind. This was the only thing which was on the mind of the Son when He came into the world. For Him, the Father was totally important and what He wanted done was all that mattered. To fulfill the Father's wishes is what gave Jesus the greatest joy even when it cost Him his life to do so. The Father was the most important person in Jesus' life. We see this from the very beginning, in the finding in the temple, when Jesus said, "Did you not know that I must be busy with my Father's affairs?" Jesus was totally in love with the Father's plans. Pleasing the Father was the most important purpose in His life: it came before pleasing His mother, or Peter, or Himself. It was more important and took priority over life itself. Jesus showed how important the Father was to Him by yielding totally to the Father. He was all space, total space for the Father. Nothing of Himself interfered with the Father's plan. In this way, He glorified the Father.

To glorify, in the New Testament, means to show up the importance of another person. Thus when Jesus revealed throughout his life, both in word and in deed, that He was totally available, totally at the disposal of His Father for the good of the world, He was glorifying the Father, showing how important He thought the Father and His wishes were. In turn, the Father showed how important the Son is: He used to watch the Son and paid attention to Him, especially through the miracle of His resurrection. The resurrection was the vindication by the Father of the attitudes of Jesus. So the Father asked everything of Jesus and Jesus was happy to respond fully with His 'Yes' which is always 'Yes' (2 Cor. 1:20). A little further on, Saint Paul says: "it is God who has shone in our minds to radiate the light of the knowledge of God's glory, the glory on the face of Christ" (2 Cor. 4:6).

In the icon, the Son is absorbed in gazing on the splendour of His Father's face. It carries Him out of Himself, He is enraptured. When we look at the Son, whether in the icon, or in the Gospels, we see the same: the Father is the object of the Son's gaze. The Son's face radiates the importance and the splendour of the Father to us. We are invited to become involved in this. The light on the Father's face shines perfectly in the Son's because the Son's face is turned totally to the Father. We, as disciples of Jesus, are meant to keep our eyes "fixed on Him" (Heb. 12-2) and so the radiance on the face of Christ begins to shine on our faces. So there is a mutual enlightening going on and, consequently, there is light for a darkened world. "We, with our unveiled faces, reflecting like mirrors the brightness of the Lord, all grow brighter and brighter as we are turned into the image that we reflect" (2 Cor. 3:18).

'Father, You always hear Me'

We said above that the delight of a lover is in granting the requests of the beloved. Jesus delighted in granting the request of the Father, that He should come to save humankind. In turn, the Father delighted in granting the requests, the prayers of His Son. So, as a human being, Jesus was confident in asking the Father for everything He needed. He told the Father what it was like to be human. He presumed that the Father would hear Him.

In the 17th chapter of Saint John's Gospel, we have the most complete prayer of Christ. He asks the Father to let Him give eternal life to all of us. He prays for us because we belong to the Father and have been given to the Son. He asks that we may be one in the same way as He and the Father are one. He wants to share all His joy with us and He asks the Father to protect us from the evil one, and to consecrate us in the truth. He asks that the world may realise that it was the Father who sent Him and that He has loved us with the same infinite love as the Father has for Him. Finally, He begs His Father that we whom the Father has given to Him may be with Him where He is. From what we have said above, we now know where the Son is: the Son is always totally present to the Father. He is totally open to the Father and He is full of the Father's love. In this sense, He is full of joy and happiness and He wishes that happiness for us. What we are invited to do is take the same stance, the same attitudes towards the Father and His designs as the Son has done.

From watching this interchange between Father and Son, we can learn much that is essential about prayer. Firstly, and most importantly, we learn that prayer begins in our knowledge of the infinite love of the Father for us and His delight in us. We too are the beloved of the Father. There is no limit to the Father's love for us. Resting in appreciation of this truth is fundamental to our prayer always. Secondly, comes our loving response: to a lover who is so good, so much on our side, wanting nothing but the best for us, wishing only to please us. To such a lover what can the response of the beloved be except to wish to do whatever the lover wants? "Behold the handmaid of the Lord; let what you have said be done to me" (Luke 1:38).

Asking in all things to please the Father will grow to be central in our prayer.

We want to be like the Son, yet we know that we fall so far short of His boundless openness to His Father. So we ask that the strength and the light and the courage may be given us, to know what the Father wants and to fulfill it. These basic attitudes in prayer, firstly, appreciating the Father's goodness to us and, secondly, desiring to respond, and asking for the grace to be able to respond, will bring us great joy and peace. To live in this way is to be joining in the conversation of the Three Divine Persons and accepting Their invitation to a place at Their table. In personal prayer and in quiet pondering over the mysteries of the life of Jesus in the Gospels and, most of all, in the liturgy, these attitudes are fostered. The Father always wants to grant our requests when they are in accord with the requests of the Son. We need the spirit of the Son in order to pray rightly and to join properly in Their conversation.

The Spirit with the Father and the Son

The Spirit is the Spirit of the Father and of the Son. He is not on His own nor is He separated from them. We can catch on to this mystery of the closeness of the relationship between the Three by thinking of a large family. The father is a good man and his wife was originally attracted to him because of his goodness and his love. In receiving and accepting him, she helps to bring out the best in him. Between them they raise a large and happy family. A visitor can see that there's a unifying spirit in the group; the goodness in the father is also in the wife and children. When one of the children responds well in a testing situation, the others say, "That's the spirit!" This indicates that the response is in harmony with the spirit of the family. Similarly, when Jesus responded rightly, as He always did to His daily challenges, the Father, delighted with Him could say, "That's the Spirit!" In one way, we cannot grasp the Spirit. We cannot see Him but we can sense Him. We know when He is with us. His role is a hidden one. We know Him by His gifts and by His fruits. He is the one who creates space in us so that the Father and Son may live in us.

The Mood of God

We have our ups and downs, and our moods fluctuate from day to day. However, the mood of the Three Divine Persons towards us is constant. It is the mood of ever faithful and unchanging love. God always feels and acts in the same way towards us and it is good to remember this when we feel low and when we fall short of responding to Them as we would wish. The Spirit expresses this final mood of the Trinity towards us. It is the mood of constant loving regard which never changes.

The Spirit is always spoken of in the New Testament as *given* to us. He is the first and best gift of the Father and Son. Good parents give their children many things and do all they can for them but, first and best of all, they give the children their love. From their love for each other, children are conceived and from that love will flow all the particular gifts they give later. Likewise, the Three are always doing Their best for us, working for us in every event and giving us

35

Themselves in a wide variety of ways. All these concrete signs of love flow from the gift of Their love which is the Holy Spirit.

The Spirit is Given

The Spirit is *fully* given to us. The donation of the Father AND the Son is unrestricted and unconditional. It is in knowing this that we have hope for the happy outcome of the dark mystery of human history. Saint Paul says that "This hope is not deceptive because the love of God has been poured into our hearts by the Holy Spirit which has been given us" (Rom. 5:5). Our part is to *receive* Him fully. Jesus commands us to "receive the Holy Spirit" (John 20:22). Another line of thought is that since we already possess Him fully, our task is to allow Him to have complete freedom of action in our hearts. We are meant to turn to Him and to listen constantly to His promptings rather than to treat Him as a forgotten guest. He is, however, self-effacing and gentle, and His mission is interior rather than exterior. His role is to touch *our* spirits and bring them into harmony with His own. While we can imagine the Father and can relate easily to the Son in His humanity, we cannot imagine or grasp the Spirit. However, we need not be upset that we cannot grasp Him. We cannot grasp our own spirits either nor are we intended to do so. Jesus compares the Spirit to the wind "which blows where it wishes" (John 3:8). Wind is free, it cannot be domesticated nor contained nor grasped. To experience the wind, we have to risk coming out from our sheltered places into the open. So, too, only when we are in the open can the Spirit move us as He wishes.

The Spirit in the World

The Spirit wants to show us the Son's beauty and the Father's tenderness and He is also accountable to Them for the completion of the work of our salvation: the gathering in of all humankind into the final community of love. He works tirelessly; He is pure energy and is infinitely resourceful. He labours in all human hearts, both in the hearts of those who acknowledge Him and in the hearts of those who don't. His goal is to draw us all into the intimacy of Divine company. He has been working in the world from the beginning because the world has always been kept lovingly in mind by God. He moved the hearts of Abraham, Moses and all the prophets. The New Testament opens with the account of Mary allowing herself to be overshadowed by the Holy Spirit. Thus, she became the first human being to be fully and unreservedly involved in the plans of God. While yet unborn, John the Baptist was prepared by the Holy Spirit for his later mission which was to announce the coming of Jesus.

The Spirit and Jesus

Jesus is revealed as the one in whom the Holy Spirit dwelt fully. The Spirit was not an impersonal force driving Jesus from outside but an inspiration, an encouragement coming from within. He was sure of Jesus and Jesus was sure of

Him. The Spirit kept the love and the intentions of the Father always before His eyes. Because the Spirit is the bond of love within the Trinity, He kept Jesus going and kept Him centred on the Father. He led Him to spend forty days in the desert and then inspired Him to begin His public life. Jesus' opening words to the world were "The Spirit of the Lord has been given to me . . . He has sent me to bring the good news to the poor, to proclaim liberty to captives and to give new sight to the blind, to set the downtrodden free, to proclaim the Lord's year of favour" (Luke 4:18).

In all He does, Jesus followed the prompting of the Spirit and so He could say "I always do what pleases the Father" (John 8:29). Jesus' greatest gift to us was the Holy Spirit. This gift was promised during His lifetime and given fully at His death. The Spirit is not left to work alone in the world while the Father and Son retire into the background. His work is Trinitarian, so He labours to point us all to the Son who in turn points us to the Father. He tries endlessly to win over our hearts that we may look at Jesus and be attracted by Him. He spotlights the Son. It is He who inspires us to read the New Testament. He attracts us to Jesus in prayer. He transforms the gifts of bread and wine so that they become the living presence of Jesus in the Eucharist. He labours to form in us the mind and attitudes of Jesus and inspires in us loving activity which is in line with the Gospels. Thus, He is always bringing us to the Table and introducing us to the Son and to the Father.

Prayer

In our prayer, the Spirit is the big Person. He is always in us. Our hearts are essentially places of prayer in which the Son and the Spirit are ceaselessly responding to the love of the Father. While we do our best to pray, it is primarily the Holy Spirit who never ceases to pray in us "with inarticulate groans", as Saint Paul says (Rom. 8:26). This prayer is our heart's treasure. We are caught up into the song which the Son and the Spirit sing to the Father. Slowly, as we mature over the years, we catch on better and better to Their song and make it our own. The Holy Spirit enables us to say 'Abba': without Him we could not say 'Father'. This ability to say 'Abba' is a wonderful gift, for it means that we are brought fully into the family relationships of the Trinity.

Liturgical prayer illustrates the fact that prayer is a divine conversation in which we are permitted to join. All liturgical prayer is addressed to the Father and it is because we are inseparably united with Christ, members of His body, that we can join in with the 'Yes' which He speaks to the Father. It is the Holy Spirit who inspires both Jesus and us to make this response. The closing words of every Eucharistic Prayer are: "Through Him, with Him and in Him, in the unity of the Holy Spirit, all glory and honour are YOURS Almighty Father". To this we respond with our 'Amen' to show that we are glad to be joined into the eternal movement of love between Father, Son and Holy Spirit.

We, Three, Come to You

Among the Three Divine Persons, *the* characteristic is that each is given over totally to the others in love. Each of Them is pointing to the others. They exist for one another, or as theologians would say, they are 'being-for-one-another'. None of Them seeks His own glory, rather each is pointing out the importance of the others and is inviting us to notice the others. The characteristic action of God is to be generous, loving, utterly self-donating. We sometimes say of a good person, "I know that that person is totally for me". This quality is a divine quality in a person, for each of the Three Divine Persons is totally for the others. The nature of God is revealed to us in this way. There is no reserve nor self-concealment by any of the Persons from the others. There is constant acceptance of the others and unfailing delight in Them.

They keep meeting one another but the meetings never become boring. There is always surprise because the expectation of seeing each other is always over-fulfilled. We often say of someone, "Well, we know so and so". We set limits in our relations with others. In the life of the Trinity there are no limits set.

Allowing Their life to take you over is a question of receiving, of noticing, of accepting, of exploring and of unfolding the gift of Their life. It is not a matter of striving but of openness to all that is already given. None of our inadequacies or sins or psychological weaknesses are so deep that the life of the Trinity is not deeper.

COSTLY LOVE

In the icon, the Three are shown with pilgrim staffs in Their hands. They are on a journey into our world. They are not remote from us but totally involved with us. They become pilgrims. It is not an easy world to enter because it is full of pain and sin. What reception can They expect? But They are not deterred. Theirs is total love, a love that is willing to be costly for them. It was the Son who came visibly into our world and Their world, but the Father and the Spirit were with Him 'all the way'. They never abandoned Him even though He felt abandoned on the Cross. They were fully involved in all He did, in all that happened to Him. He was sure of Them and trusted fully in Their love to sustain Him to the end.

A Human Heart

This costly love is one of the deepest mysteries of God. We can only ask humbly that something of it be revealed to us. We cannot penetrate it fully. The cost began to be paid in the Incarnation. The Son freely lay aside the glory of being God, of being equal in majesty to the Father and the Spirit. For Him to become human was like a king becoming a slave. He emptied Himself. Saint Paul tells us "to empty is to have nothing for oneself; it is a form of death" (Phil. 2:7). The Son did this in pure love but it was costly. Only tremendous love could have risked this and known that all would work out somehow.

Emptied, then, of all that He had known, the Son came to us and asked to be received and accepted. He left the table of the Trinity, as it were, He left the security of His own home, His element, to seek a home with us who share a common humanity with Him. We did not know Him nor did we accept Him. He was rejected, an outcast. The Light came into the darkness but the darkness had no eye for the Light. Through taking on a human heart the Son became vulnerable: the Trinity could now be 'got at' in a frightening way in the Son. They could be wounded, pained, even killed. We often avoid becoming involved because of the fear of rejection. It is one of the most painful of human experiences. The Trinity risked Their love totally and found it rejected, despised. Their steadiness in continuing to love cost Them everything.

His Heart, an Open Wound of Love

The Cross was the climax, the dramatic presentation for all to see, of this costly love. Here the Father gave over the Son into our hands, into the hands of humanity, in anguished love to show that He wanted to withhold nothing from us. "Since God did not spare His own Son, but gave Him up for us all, we may be certain, after such a gift, that He will not refuse anything He can give" (Rom. 8:32). To give over to us what was most precious to Him was costly love for the Father.

There is a sense in which the Father and the Spirit lost the Son in the Passion. Saint Paul speaks of the Son 'becoming sin'. Sin means being distanced from God, being alienated. We can say that Jesus was lost, out of his element, when he assumed our sin so fully. He became the Prodigal Son who found himself in a far country, distant and separated forever, as it seemed, from the joy and happiness of His Father's home and love. Thus, the Son identifies with us in our sin.

The Father and Spirit were still with Him in His exile but Jesus did not experience Their presence. He was not consoled by Them. He felt totally abandoned. Only the thread of blind trust held him, so that He could still pray even when He sensed that He was forsaken: "My God, my God, why have you deserted me?" (Mt. 27:47).

All our 'whys?' are taken up in the 'why?' of Jesus. He identifies with you in the 'whys?' of your life. On the Cross, the Father and the Spirit were close by. In fact, They were holding Him but Jesus could not feel Their presence. In our lives, too, this is so often the case. We feel abandoned by God but, in fact, They are holding us. It is because of this costly love, this total identification with us in everything, that we become brothers and sisters of Jesus. He goes with us all the way. Thus He can bring us by the hand to our place at the table. We are now 'in Christ Jesus'.

The early Church took the parable of the Good Samaritan to refer to Jesus travelling in search of lost humanity and finding us robbed of our dignity, and half dead by the roadside of history. He pours on the oil and wine, and carries us on His own back to the inn (which represents the Church) and commands that we be taken care of. As the Father's only Son, and as the true Atlas, He took

39

the world upon His shoulders.

Now when the Trinity look on us, They see us bound inseparately to the Son. He is the elder brother, the first-born of many brothers and sisters, who adopts us and brings us into His own family and home.

'Into Your Hands I Commend My Spirit'

The Father gave over the Son in total love and the Son allowed Himself to be given over. He gave Himself over to the Father's plans and in so doing, gave Himself over to us. Then it was the turn of the Spirit to be given over, the Spirit of love that sealed Their life. The only possession that Jesus had at the end of His life was His spirit, the Holy Spirit. We can say that He never lost His Spirit even in the darkest hour of the Cross. The Spirit remained true to Him, constant and steadfast in His love. To reveal the utter limits of His love, the Son gave His very Spirit back to His Father. The Spirit was His faithful companion. Now He allowed Himself to be sent into the Father's hands. There is a promise in this. The Spirit is now free to be given to everyone. He comes to us, sent by the Father and the Son, as the final gift which was yet the first gift. He comes with power and His mission is to transform our hearts until they are like the heart of the Son. The Spirit is untiring in His efforts, totally faithful. He works with infinite love. All, now, is given over to us; the cost is fully paid but the love outweighs the cost.

And We?

We are invited to ponder, contemplate, reverence and praise this costly love of the Three. They are not only Three Persons fully given over to each other in joyous love but they are given over to us too in the same unrestricted way. Reflect on some cross in your own life and try to let yourself be open to the truth that They are with you, behind you, wishing the best for you and trying to make it happen. In this way, you may find deeper meanings behind the surface of life. 'God is very good'. Many people come to see this despite all the sufferings they endure. This is a knowledge born of awareness of Their steady and constant love in the midst of all sorts of difficulties.

Because of Their total involvement with us, we are caught up into Their world and into Their love. This implies that our love will be costly too. In the face of evil and suffering in the world, we are called to be with Them, for They are identified with the poor, the broken, the despised and unwanted people of this world. They will show us what we have to do, as Jesus was shown by the Spirit. Insofar as we are willing to risk ourselves as They did, we form part of that growing community of persons rooted in eternity, who labour to bring the world to rights. The Three, then, delight in us, embrace us, recognise us as Their own.

No matter how vast evil seems to be, love extends wider. Infinite love is astir in the world and whatever the cost demanded in winning over our hearts, even death itself, love is willing to pay. "The cost is reckoned, the enterprise is

40

begun, it cannot be withstood", said Edmund Campion facing martyrdom at Tyburn.

Reflect on ways in which you have shown love in situations where the costs were great. We talk about a 'labour of love'. The cost might be great but your love goes far beyond the cost and, perhaps, you don't even realise it. Think of those people who look after sick or elderly members of their families. They spend hours on end with them and, perhaps, lose out on their sleep. There is a great amount of cost here but the love for the sick or elderly person outweighs this cost. Did you ever walk a great distance to find the right present for someone you love? There is cost there, too, but usually the miles of walking are forgotten about because of the joy of the love that is there. Similarly, with the Trinity, love wins out and eclipses the tremendous cost.

THE EUCHARIST

They take the Initiative

In each of the Sacraments we meet the Trinity, or rather, They take the initiative and come to meet us. We often forget Them but They keep us always in mind. In the Eucharist, we come to the table of the Trinity in a most profound way. Here They meet us most fully and most openly. It is a celebration of our relationship with Them as a community, while also showing infinite respect for us as individuals through our receiving Christ personally in Communion. The Eucharist is a preview of that final community of love in which all people will fully rejoice. It is a gathering of persons both divine and human, to celebrate the mystery that underpins all our history, the mystery of divine love which will ultimately transform what is now painful and tragic into everlasting joy. They lay the table, as it were. They take over. The Son offers Himself to the Father in the perfect offering, the Spirit changes the bread and wine into the Body and Blood of the Son. We are invited to come and be transformed.

Source and Summit

Vatican II speaks of the Eucharist as the source and summit of Christian life. The manner in which the liturgy is celebrated may be boring and unsatisfying but deep down the Eucharist is the most dynamic event that occurs in our world. All the loving energy of God is focussed on this moment. Of all the mysteries we have touched on in this booklet, this is by far the greatest: it best expresses God's love for us. It can only be appreciated within the mystery of the Trinity: it begins and ends by calling on Them. It celebrates the Father's infinite love for us in giving us His Son; it reveals the wholehearted response of the Son to the Father's plans. The Spirit which is the bond of unity between Father and Son, here gathers us into unity with Them. He opens our hearts to appreciate the Son and to respond as the Son did to the requests of the Father. Thus He teaches us to be for others. Just as divine love is focussed outward, likewise we are to be given over to others in their need. The redemption of the world is carried on through us according as we embody this love in our lives.

Extravagance

The icon illustrates that we are invited to take our special place at the table of the Trinity. We are not alone: the space is for the whole world. At this banqueting table nothing is spared, not even the only Son. Everything is a gift. There is divine extravagance here. The prayers of the Eucharist reflect this lavish nature of Their love: 'Always and everywhere . . . *All* holiness . . . from east to west . . . from age to age . . . *All* life . . .".

The words reflect the length and breadth, the height and depth of Their love and Their concern. The words of the Consecration are very simple but they speak of total giving and undivided love: "This is my Body . . . this is my Blood". The gesture is extravagant. Rich liturgical music such as Beethoven's *Missa Solemnis* catches something of this extravagance in a way that words cannot. From the opening words of the Mass, it is clear that nothing will be withheld from us: "All is gift; the grace of Our Lord Jesus Christ, the love of the Father and the companionship of the Holy Spirit". Everything that is of ultimate value is given.

Our Gift

In the face of such unconditional love, we are asked to be open and receptive. Our openness is our first gift. When you love someone, nothing is more frustrating than their refusing to accept your love. We must not grieve the Holy Spirit in this way. We are invited to allow ourselves to be loved totally by the Three.

The Eucharist is the perfect prayer of Jesus to His Father and we are invited to add our 'Yes' to His. His life was a living out of His statement: "I always do what pleases Him" (John 8:29). That made His whole life a prayer. Although we lose courage when faced with demands that can be made of us, the Eucharist makes that prayer for us. Prayer is, first of all, the conversation of the Trinity and this prayer is in us, beyond our knowing it, because of the life of the Three in us. We need to pray that this life of Theirs may gain more and more ground in us, so that eventually we become as Jesus was: all space for Their activity. Then there will be one Christ: all people saying 'Yes' to the Father's plans.

With Empty Hands

We come to the Eucharist with empty hands, needy and hungry for the best gift of God which is Himself. We are like the people in the Gospels who came in droves to Jesus and asked for what they wanted: "If you want to, you can cure me" (Mark 1:40); "Let me see again" (Luke 18:41); "I implore you to look at my son" (Luke 9:38). The woman with the haemorrhage said: "If I can touch even his clothes I shall be well again" (Mark 5:28).

We have much more intimate contact with the Lord in the Eucharist. Because of the faith of these people and of their openness to receive, they obtained the things they wanted. Do we believe enough in His love to ask for what we need most? In fact, what we need most, though we may not know it, is God Himself. Therefore, we must beg that They, who dwell deep within us, may be liberated and take us over. Thus we can live out the rest of our lives 'under new management'. They want this because it is the best for us but we must want it too. There is great love in our crying out to Them from our hearts, especially after Communion. One of the saddest things that could happen, when we meet Them face to face, would be to have Them say, "You never asked us for anything!" This can help us to trust Them enough and to allow Them unhindered play in our lives.

Cosmic Joy

Because we sin, there is a problem of evil but, because God is so good, there is a solution to it. We do not see the solution fully yet but we shall. "All will be well" (Julian of Norwich).

We have tried to indicate the master-strokes of the solution. The details are still hidden but they need not dismay us. The Three Divine Persons have opened wide Their doors and have invited all of us to enter and sit at table with Them. How this is to be worked out is unclear to us but not to Them. If you go to a huge party, you may well wonder how the hosts will cope with the large crowd or how they will deal with unexpected emergencies, especially with difficult people. When the hosts are divine, you can be sure they can manage. Julian of Norwich was puzzled as to how the Lord could promise that all would be well at the end; she could not see how the cosmic party could be a success if the preparations were so disastrous. Neither can we. Finally, the thought came to her: on the Last Day, the Blessed Trinity will perform a deed through which Their goodness and love would finally triumph. "They who made all from nothing shall make well all that is not well" (Rev. 32).

AT THE TABLE IN DAILY LIFE

If we can accept in faith that God will not fail the world He loves so dearly, then we can turn to ourselves and sum up the attitudes we need to cultivate, so that They may find us to be part of the solution rather than part of the problem.

Attentiveness

I need to consider what They think of me. Can I accept that They love me unconditionally, just as I am? Can I accept that I can come to the Table shabby, worn out and ashamed, and that I will find Them looking on me "lovingly and humbly", as Saint Teresa says. Can I allow each of Them in turn to kiss me and hug me with joy, as the father does in the parable of the Prodigal Son?

There are two stories of me: Theirs and mine. Mine is built up over the years from what others say of me and what I say of myself. As the years go on, the less appealing it may become. Then there is Their story of me. It began before the world was made, when I was chosen to live through love in Their presence. It is full of hope and stretches out into a limitless and glorious future. It becomes better and better, even as I move into old age, and death looms up. To Them I am no ordinary mortal; I am immortal and totally precious. I must listen to Their story of myself rather than my own. I must pray for the grace to listen well to what the most significant Persons in my life are trying to tell me. Then, also, I can listen to what They say about my neighbours, rather than linger on *my* story of them.

Perfect Harmony

We noted that Saint Ignatius of Loyola had a revelation of the Trinity as three musical notes in harmony. Can I find my note within Their chord? I need to grow in sensitivity to the difference between harmony and disharmony. Imagine a good musician having to listen to someone who hasn't a note in their head. I need to ask Them to play Their music in me. By watching the Son and by taking on His values and attitudes, my life becomes integrated into Theirs and becomes more simple. As T.S. Eliot says: "A condition of complete simplicity costs no less than everything".

Jesus' life was very simple. It was exclusively focussed on His Father's business which was, and is, summed up as "bringing us to where They are" (John 14:3, 17:24). For me, there is the ongoing struggle to surrender my personal dreams, even though they grow so tattered and shabby and restricting. Let me give my consent to the mysterious dreams of the Three for me, for these alone offer me space enough to grow to be my full self. Only Their dreams are big enough for the world's needs, for the limitless aspirations and desires of each man and woman on our fair yet wounded planet.

What has been sketched out here are the outlines of a divine love affair. The plot is complex. All the characters, even the most unsuitable ones, are being wooed by God in mysterious love but most do not know it. For those who know it and accept it, life is changed and they play their part in wooing the rest, by creating around themselves a loving and inviting atmosphere in which a person can grow. Theirs is a love like God's: always open, ready, energetic in building bridges across the chasms that divide people from one another. It is a love that sets no limit to the cost it is willing to pay. Those who have caught on, who have been caught, are strengthened and mutually supported by the Christian community where the Three have full scope for Their loving designs. The members are encouraged in their work by knowing that the Spirit is alive and active *incognito,* playing on seemingly closed hearts and darkened consciences. They know, too, that the Son endlessly intercedes before His Father for the members of His body, all of them: "I will draw *everyone* to me" (John 12:32). And the Father? They know that He, the Maker of all Harmony, works to draw music even from the most discordant notes, and to fashion them beyond the intentions of their authors, into Eternal Harmony.

Intercession

The more I catch on to this music, the more do divine concerns become mine. They take over my life. There is a dance going on and I am watching it but I'm not left to sit like a wallflower. They catch me by the hand and draw me in. I don't have the rhythm quite right for a while but it grows on me. They leave one of my hands free to catch and draw in someone else. So by being with Them at Their table and by being caught up into Their dance, I influence those around me, for I am united with them in a common bond of humanity and destiny. My life with Them brings life to others. None of my experiences need be wasted. None of them fails to touch others whether they be my responses to grace or my sinning. I can support others as they support me, often unknowingly but none the less really. My sufferings, when patiently accepted, purify me and others too, as Jesus' sufferings purified us all. "I make up in my body what is wanting" (Col. 1:24). All our lives touch at this deep level. There is one body, partly healthy and growing partly sick and dying, but one body. Let me do all that I can out of love for all. Let me endure what must be endured, again for love of all. Let me pray and worship, not just for myself but for all. We are delegates of prayer for the world. One who prays, prays for the world.

We are never alone. We are at the Table. Beside us are all our brothers and sisters who have caught on and have accepted the invitation. Behind us stand the silent, unseeing multitudes. They press against us, squeeze us. leave us feeling uncomfortable until we secure them a place at the Table. They hunger and thirst for what would make them happy. I cannot block them from the Table. I must stand up and make space. Before I have a chance to sit down again in comfort, I feel another tip my shoulder and a voice pleading: "Let me in, let me in!" We carry the world as Jesus carried it. To paraphrase Pascal, we are all in agony until the end, when a place at Table will have been found for all. Our hearts have to grow and become ever more spacious like the all-embracing love of the Trinity. Their love is expansive. The circumference of the Table is not limited; it expands to hold everyone. It is a round table to emphasise the quality of all the guests. "No before, or after; a circle without bound; the centre, Everywhere" (Zen).

They collected together everyone they could find,
good and bad alike;
and the wedding hall was filled with guests.
May it be so! May our lives make it so! Amen.

Glory be to the Father
And to the Son
And to the Holy Spirit.
As it was in the beginning is now and ever shall be
World without end.